THIS BOOK BELONGS TO:

Hello!

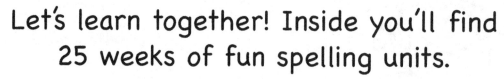

Let's learn together! Inside you'll find 25 weeks of fun spelling units.

Each unit will have 4 practice pages.

Remember to:

1. **Look at each spelling word**
2. **Say the word out loud**
3. **Write the word**
4. **Have tons of fun!**

Don't forget to check your spelling of each word after you've finished.

DIGITAL ANSWER KEY

Found at the back of the book

SPELLING WORDS

1. lunch
2. list
3. balloon
4. barn
5. piece
6. wool
7. might
8. pail
9. short
10. notebook

**Trace the word on the left,
then write it two more times on the right.**

1. Circle the correctly spelled words
2. Rewrite the incorrect words on the lines to the left

① _____	lunch	pail	wull
② _____	short	piece	might
③ _____	list	nottebook	ballloon

Draw a line to connect the matching words

lunch	wool
list	lunch
barn	piece
piece	barn
wool	list

Put all of the spelling words in alphabetical order

1. _____
2. _____
3. _____
4. _____
5. _____
6. _____
7. _____
8. _____
9. _____
10. _____

Unscramble the words and write the correct spelling on the line

ecpei _____

hgtim _____

torhs _____

llnoabo _____

Write the correct spelling for each image

_____

To do:

_____

FIND EACH OF THE SPELLING WORDS IN THE WORDSEARCH BELOW

S	Z	O	C	I	S	C	N	I	W	Z	R
B	V	M	O	K	H	O	A	O	E	Y	R
G	N	S	I	S	O	M	O	B	F	S	F
V	O	O	I	L	R	L	L	S	K	T	G
D	T	Z	L	T	T	U	X	H	J	T	J
K	E	A	S	T	N	Y	F	J	S	F	Y
T	B	T	O	C	R	V	Z	I	F	Z	P
E	O	Y	H	D	A	S	L	T	L	P	F
J	O	P	W	G	B	B	F	U	G	H	L
R	K	C	A	T	I	L	Q	R	T	G	G
S	P	I	J	I	E	M	L	S	C	J	V
Z	C	S	F	X	L	E	C	E	I	P	B

LUNCH

LIST

BALLOON

BARN

PIECE

WOOL

MIGHT

PAIL

SHORT

NOTEBOOK

Under each picture write the correct spelling of each word

_____   _____   _____

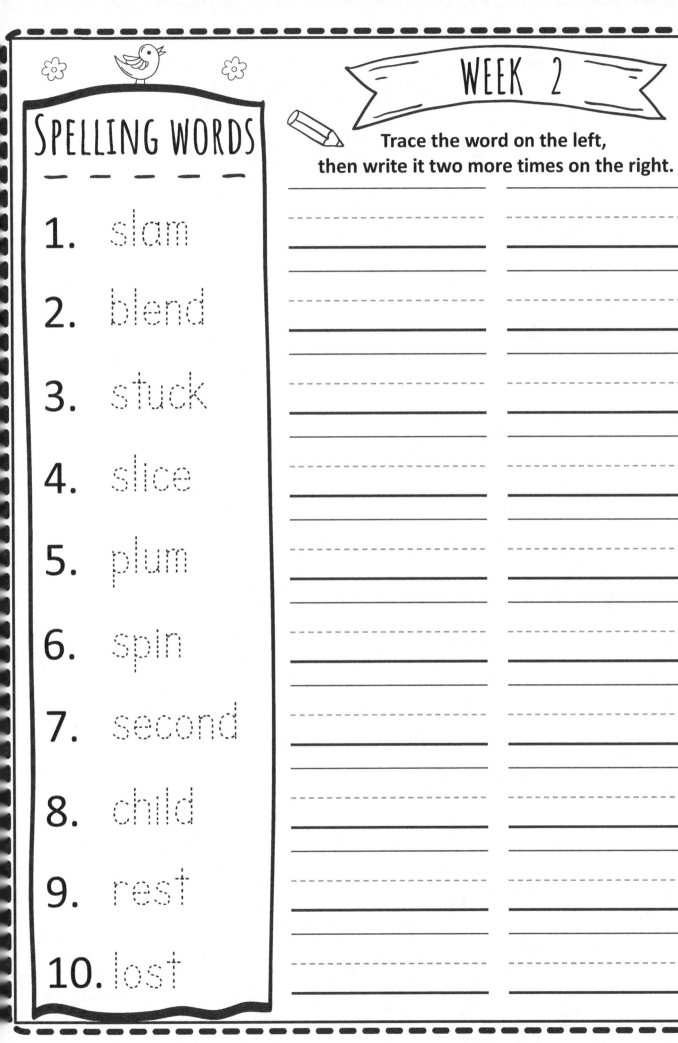

WEEK 2

Spelling Words

1. slam
2. blend
3. stuck
4. slice
5. plum
6. spin
7. second
8. child
9. rest
10. lost

Trace the word on the left,
then write it two more times on the right.

WRITE EACH SPELLING WORD IN THE ROCKETS BELOW

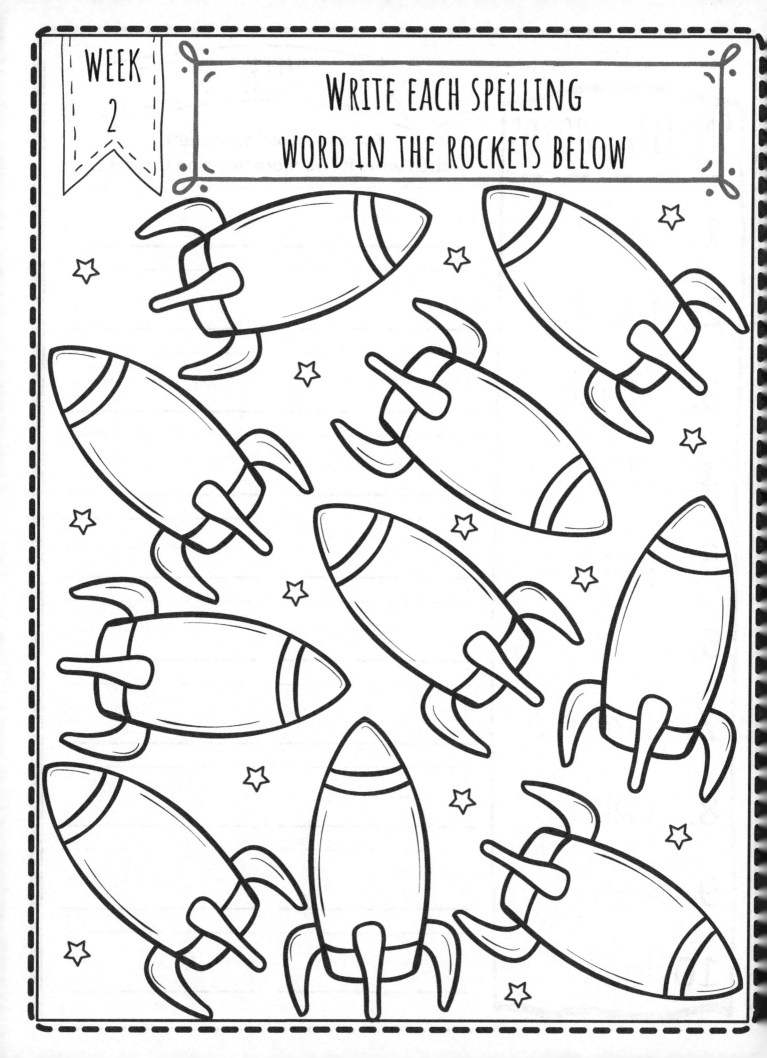

Use the letters to complete the word. Some letters can be used more than once. Make sure to trace the full word.

d e l s o i h n k

_____   _____

s _ c _ d   t u c

b l   c _ d

Put the following words in the correct shape boxes

rest   slam   slice

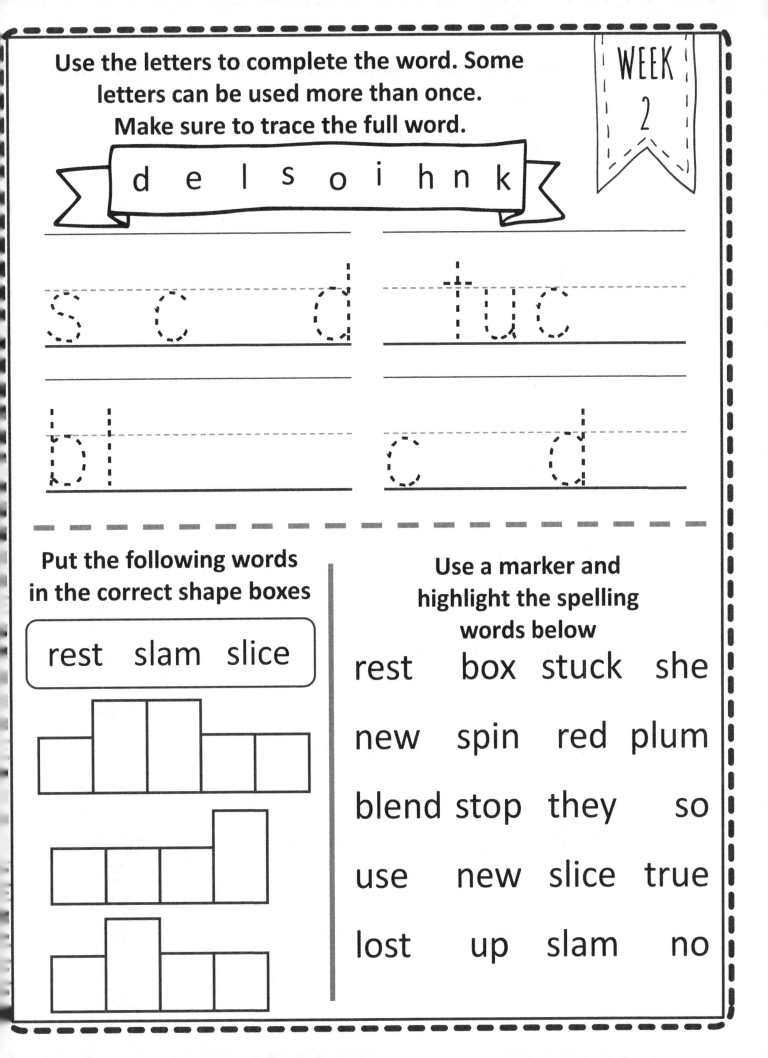

Use a marker and highlight the spelling words below

rest   box   stuck   she

new   spin   red   plum

blend   stop   they   so

use   new   slice   true

lost   up   slam   no

Use the words below to complete the sentences.

second   child   slam   blend   stuck
lost   rest   slice

Please wait one _____ , I need to _____ .

Do not _____ the door.

I did not win, I _____ .

Can you help me _____ some cheese?

I am not an adult, I am a _____ .

The car is _____ in the mud.

Use a brush to _____ the colors.

SPELLING WORDS

Trace the word on the left, then write it two more times on the right.

1. everywhere
2. tribe
3. prime
4. dish
5. crank
6. trade
7. weak
8. song
9. light
10. carry

THIS RABBIT LOVES ICE CREAM. HELP HIM WRITE A SPELLING WORD IN EACH SCOOP, THEN COLOR THEM!

Put the following words in their correct shape boxes

weak song dish

WEEK 3

Use the clues below to fill out the crossword with spelling words

1. Not dark

2. To buy or sell

3. Hold and move

4. Eat on this

5. Not strong

6. Group of people

7. In all places

8. Turn this

9. Best quality

10. Sing this

WEEK 3

Circle this week's correct spelling word in each row

1. trybe   triibe   tribe   tribee

2. primee   preme   pryme   prime

3. carry   carey   carri   carrie

4. seng   song   ssong   songg

Use the words below to complete the sentences

carry   trade   crank   everywhere

There is dirt _____ !

Turn the _____ to open it.

Let's _____ some candy.

Can you help me _____ my book?

SPELLING WORDS

Trace the word on the left,
then write it two more times on the right.

1. bedroom

2. count

3. brick

4. die

5. deer

6. state

7. bunch

8. grind

9. desk

10. tell

WEEK 4

Draw a line to connect the matching words

desk	bedroom
deer	deer
grind	desk
bedroom	tell
tell	grind

Write the spelling word that best matches each of the images

1...2...3...

_____

_____

_____

_____

FIND EACH SPELLING WORD IN THE WORDSEARCH BELOW

WEEK 4

D	M	L	B	C	W	W	K	B	P	F	G
E	U	O	Q	D	P	C	C	N	A	K	K
S	Y	M	O	E	I	D	H	O	T	U	Y
K	B	H	U	R	Q	R	C	J	U	P	W
N	C	J	B	N	D	E	N	R	I	N	R
E	V	S	M	F	W	E	U	P	V	S	T
Q	G	K	T	U	K	D	B	P	D	K	U
M	O	H	D	A	L	P	F	M	R	X	E
E	G	R	V	Y	T	L	N	E	X	N	L
P	U	Y	W	T	T	E	E	P	I	P	L
B	R	S	D	J	L	O	D	T	V	O	U
F	Z	O	F	I	D	N	I	R	G	I	M

DESK

COUNT

BRICK

DIE

DEER

STATE

BUNCH

GRIND

BEDROOM

TELL

Put the following words in their correct shape boxes

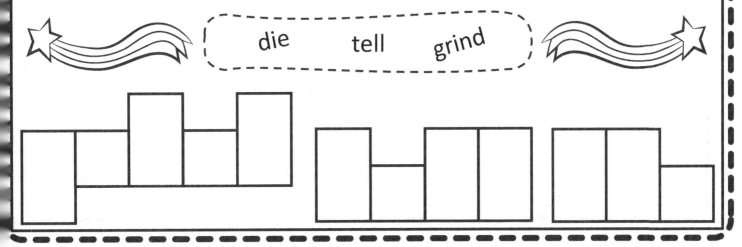

die   tell   grind

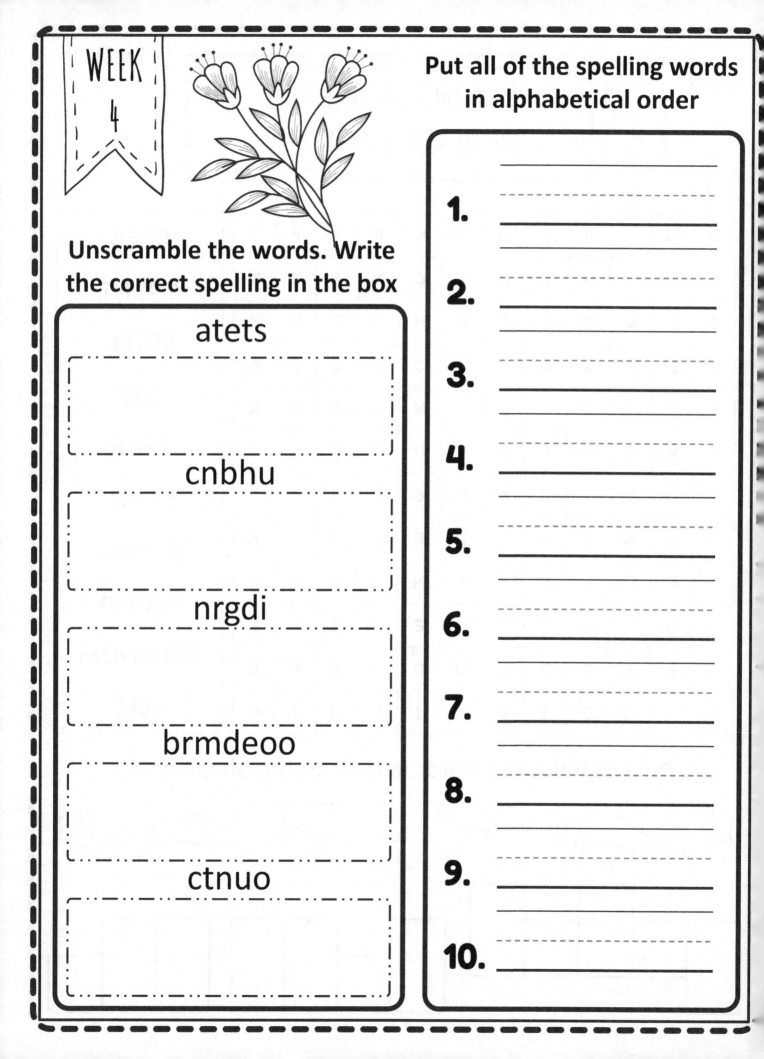

Put all of the spelling words in alphabetical order

Unscramble the words. Write the correct spelling in the box

atets

cnbhu

nrgdi

brmdeoo

ctnuo

1.

2.

3.

4.

5.

6.

7.

8.

9.

10.

SPELLING WORDS

Trace the word on the left, then write it two more times on the right.

1. lunchroom
2. shook
3. stack
4. does
5. crow
6. chicken
7. everyone
8. grass
9. loaf
10. nobody

Use the key to find the hidden spelling words

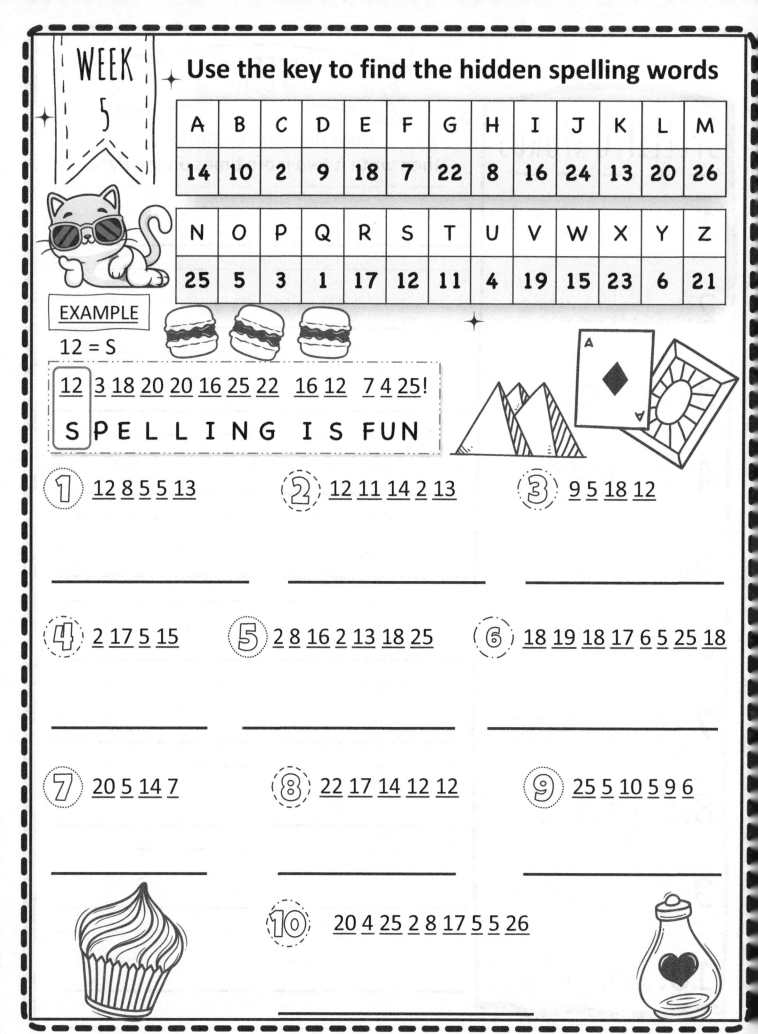

A	B	C	D	E	F	G	H	I	J	K	L	M
14	10	2	9	18	7	22	8	16	24	13	20	26

N	O	P	Q	R	S	T	U	V	W	X	Y	Z
25	5	3	1	17	12	11	4	19	15	23	6	21

EXAMPLE

12 = S

12 3 18 20 20 16 25 22   16 12   7 4 25!

S P E L L I N G   I S   F U N

① 12 8 5 5 13

② 12 11 14 2 13

③ 9 5 18 12

④ 2 17 5 15

⑤ 2 8 16 2 13 18 25

⑥ 18 19 18 17 6 5 25 18

⑦ 20 5 14 7

⑧ 22 17 14 12 12

⑨ 25 5 10 5 9 6

⑩ 20 4 25 2 8 17 5 5 26

Help Teddy write a spelling word in each piece of candy. Then color each one!

Circle all of the letters in each spelling word

stack	v s n k i f a c t y q
does	e d z o a y b d t n s
chicken	k l t d c q a e t h n i
grass	s d g i a u r d f s a
nobody	y d m s o f a n o m b

Put the following words in their correct shape boxes

shook nobody crow

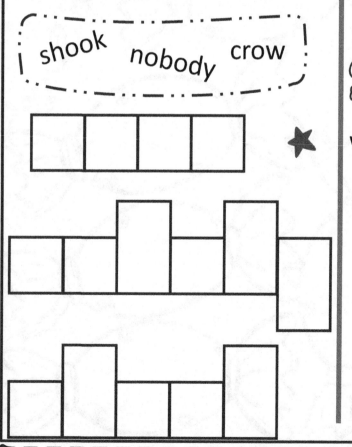

Circle the spelling words to help the rabbit get the carrot

stack	shook	help
wit	fit	does
wow	loaf	lunchroom	crow
fly	chicken	ice	hit
eat	nine	everyone	tie
fire	that	grass	sun
stop	nice	nobody

SPELLING WORDS

Trace the word on the left,
then write it two more times on the right.

1. children
2. kitten
3. meal
4. very
5. front
6. bait
7. person
8. plus
9. trail
10. spark

FIND EACH SPELLING WORD IN THE WORDSEARCH BELOW

A	J	Z	H	P	E	A	O	M	X	C	C
F	R	O	N	T	D	R	F	U	L	H	M
J	R	G	C	F	H	G	K	J	U	I	V
P	Y	J	C	F	S	K	B	W	L	L	M
E	X	N	F	H	U	B	J	I	V	D	Q
R	E	T	E	S	A	Z	A	V	O	R	S
S	P	Q	K	T	U	R	O	I	M	E	U
O	Z	O	I	S	T	Q	V	V	T	N	L
N	M	P	P	T	M	I	G	E	N	R	P
T	I	A	X	X	E	V	K	Y	R	T	W
A	R	X	B	V	A	Z	R	J	I	Y	F
K	L	K	Y	O	L	C	A	B	U	F	A

KITTEN

MEAL

CHILDREN

VERY

FRONT

BAIT

PERSON

PLUS

TRAIL

SPARK

Choose three words from the spelling list and write them below. Color each letter of the word with a different color.

_____   _____

Start at any letter and move around the circle, forward or backward, to find one of the spelling words. Circle the first letter then write the full word below

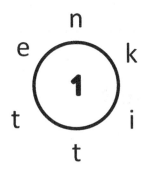

n
e **1** k
t i
t

c
h n
i **2** e
r
l d

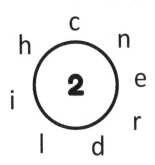

_____   _____

s
o r
n **3** e
p

a
p r
s **4** k

n
t o
f **5** r

_____   _____   _____

Circle this week's correct spelling word in each row

1. meel   meele   meal   meale

2. traiil   traail   treyl   trail

3. bait   bate   baate   bayte

4. veery   very   verie   varri

Use the words below to complete the sentences

person   meal   bait   kitten   very

My favorite _____ is breakfast.

Today it is _____ hot and windy outside!

Baby cats are called _____ .

Worms are good _____ for fishing.

I am a good _____ .

Unscramble the words and write the correct spelling on the line

prska _____

aitb _____

yrve _____

einldcrh _____

fnotr _____

ulsp _____

lmae _____

larti _____

SPELLING WORDS

Trace the word on the left, then write it two more times on the right.

1. yesterday
2. found
3. house
4. jump
5. cross
6. happy
7. lean
8. shark
9. drove
10. rust

WEEK 7

Can you help Toast Kitty write a spelling word on each piece of paper?

Write the correct spelling for each image

← today

① _____

③ _____

② _____

④ _____

1. Circle the correctly spelled words
2. Rewrite the incorrect words on the lines to the left

① _____

② _____

③ _____

④ _____

ruust	drove	sharke
lean	happi	cross
jump	found	yisterday

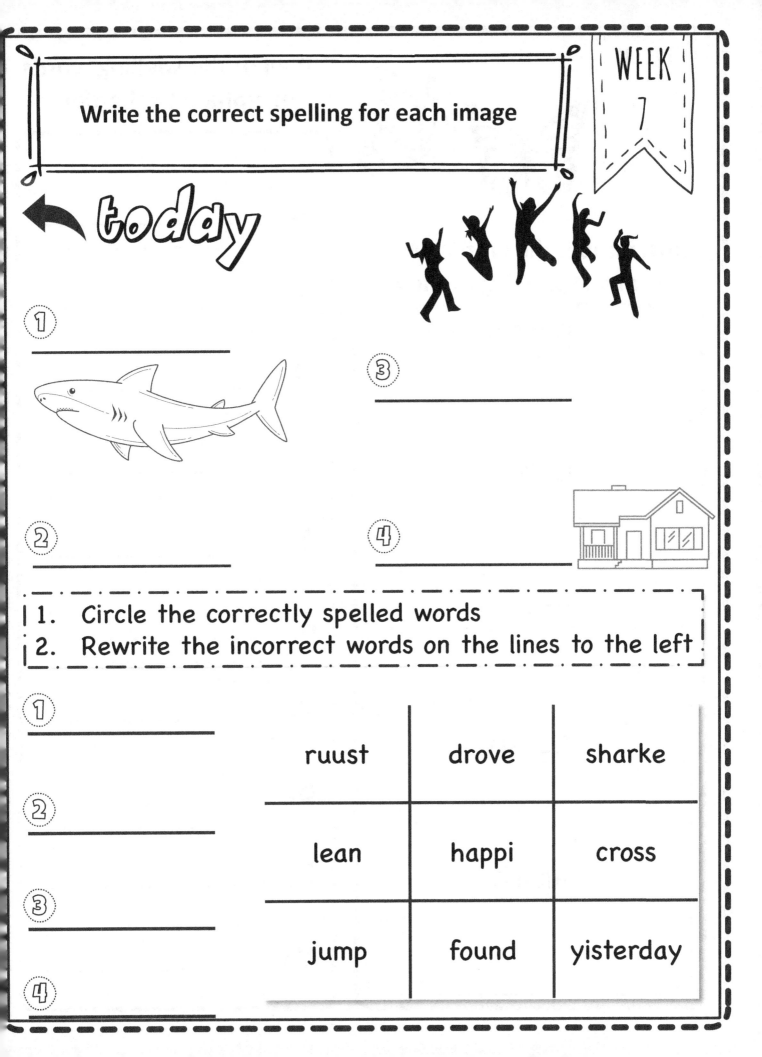

Put all of the spelling words in alphabetical order

Unscramble the words. Write the correct spelling in the box

payph

uehso

fdnuo

eovrd

aksrh

1.

2.

3.

4.

5.

6.

7.

8.

9.

10.

SPELLING WORDS

Trace the word on the left,
then write it two more times on the right.

1. twelve
2. friend
3. wind
4. uncle
5. slide
6. upon
7. dream
8. share
9. busy
10. blaze

WEEK 8

Use the clues below to fill out the crossword with spelling words

Across

3. When air moves

4. A parent's brother

5. Having a lot to do

7. Someone you can rely on

9. To give a piece of

Down

1. Once _____ a time

2. One more than eleven

5. A large fire

6. This is fun to go down

8. When you sleep

Use the letters to complete the word.
Some letters can be used more than once.
Make sure to trace the full word.

d e l s o i h n k

w i e _ e   _ r e d

_ z e _   _ d _ _ m

Use a marker and highlight the spelling words below

wind   box   busy   slide

new   blaze   red   plum

share   upon   they   uncle

dream   new   slice   true

lost twelve   make   blue

Put the following words in the correct shape boxes

dream *wind* busy

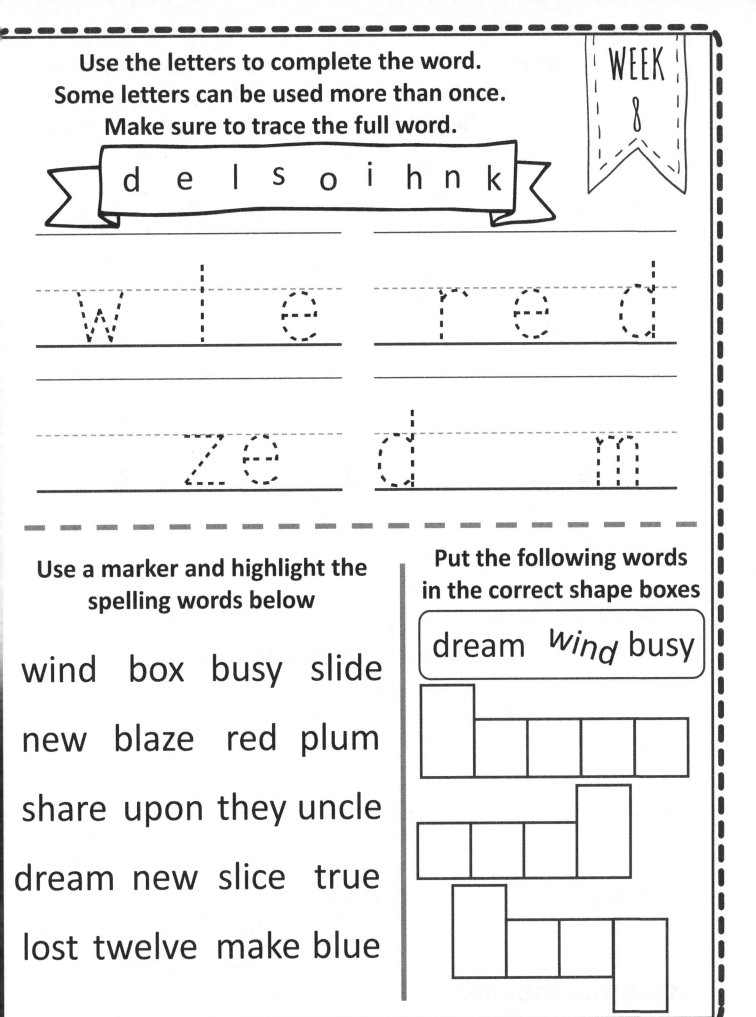

Start at any letter and move around the circle, forward or backward, to find one of the spelling words. Circle the first letter then write the full word below

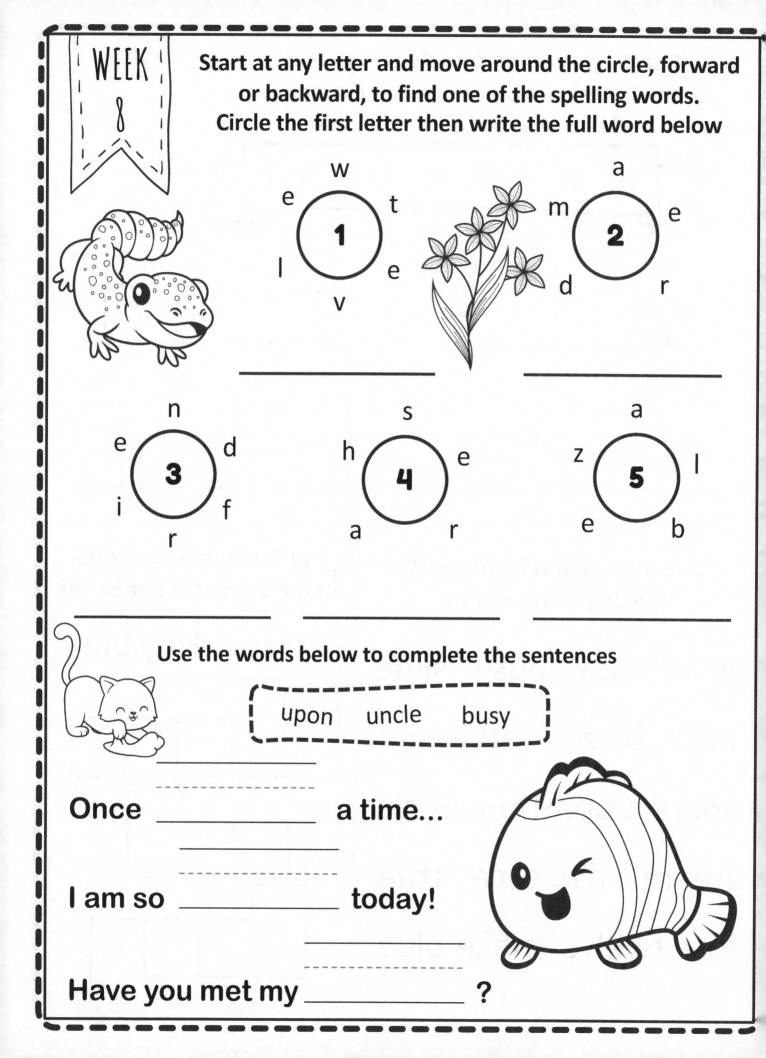

1. w t e e l v

2. a m e d r

3. n e d i f r

4. s h e a r

5. a z l e b

_____ _____ _____

Use the words below to complete the sentences

upon   uncle   busy

_____

Once _____ a time...

I am so _____ today!

Have you met my _____ ?

SPELLING WORDS

Trace the word on the left,
then write it two more times on the right.

1. because

2. lion

3. trick

4. wait

5. buy

6. speak

7. dye

8. notes

9. sheer

10. pull

Put all of the spelling words in alphabetical order

Unscramble the words. Write the correct spelling in the box

itckr

taiw

ekpsa

eebcsau

ionl

1.

2.

3.

4.

5.

6.

7.

8.

9.

10.

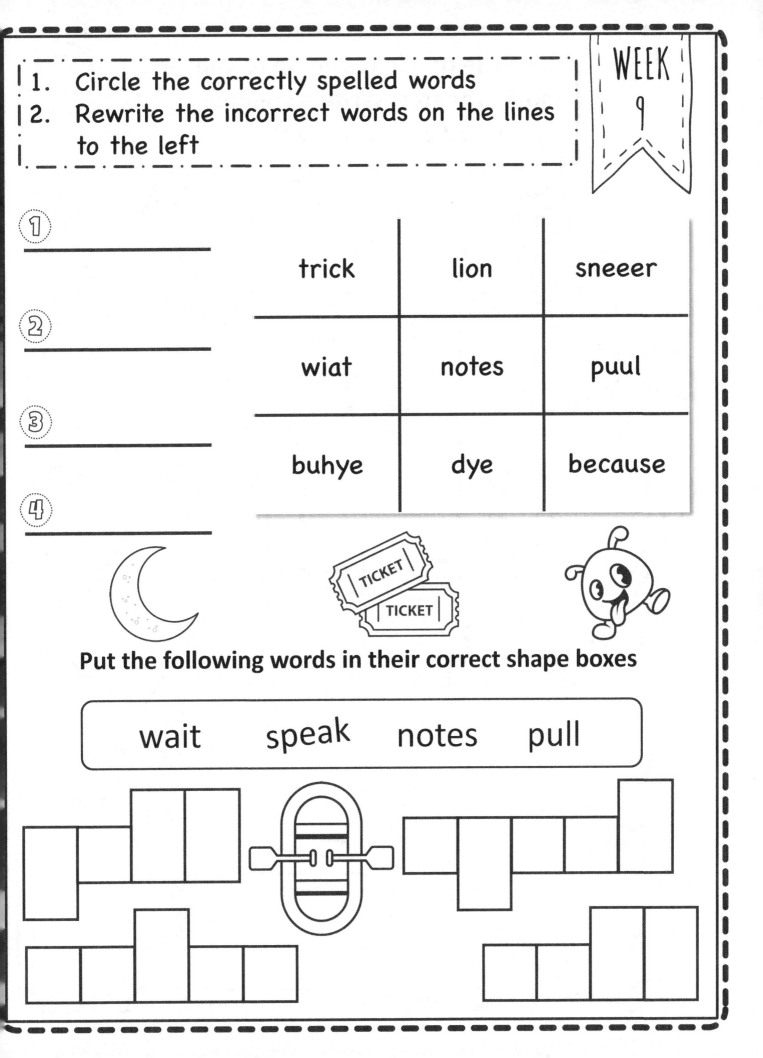

1. Circle the correctly spelled words
2. Rewrite the incorrect words on the lines to the left

① _____

② _____

③ _____

④ _____

trick	lion	sneeer
wiat	notes	puul
buhye	dye	because

Put the following words in their correct shape boxes

wait   speak   notes   pull

This little dog loves going to the movie theater. Write a spelling word on each ticket.

SPELLING WORDS

Trace the word on the left,
then write it two more times on the right.

1. grandmother

2. right

3. pine

4. went

5. slick

6. chest

7. fast

8. mitt

9. jam

10. sleek

Draw a line to connect the matching words

slick	sleek
sleek	slick
fast	jam
mitt	fast
jam	mitt

Circle all of the letters in each spelling word

slick	v s l k i f s c g t y i v t
mitt	e d t m o a y i d t n q
grandmother	o m t d e r a r t h n g
fast	s d g t a u r d f s a t z
sleek	y l m s o f e n o e k b

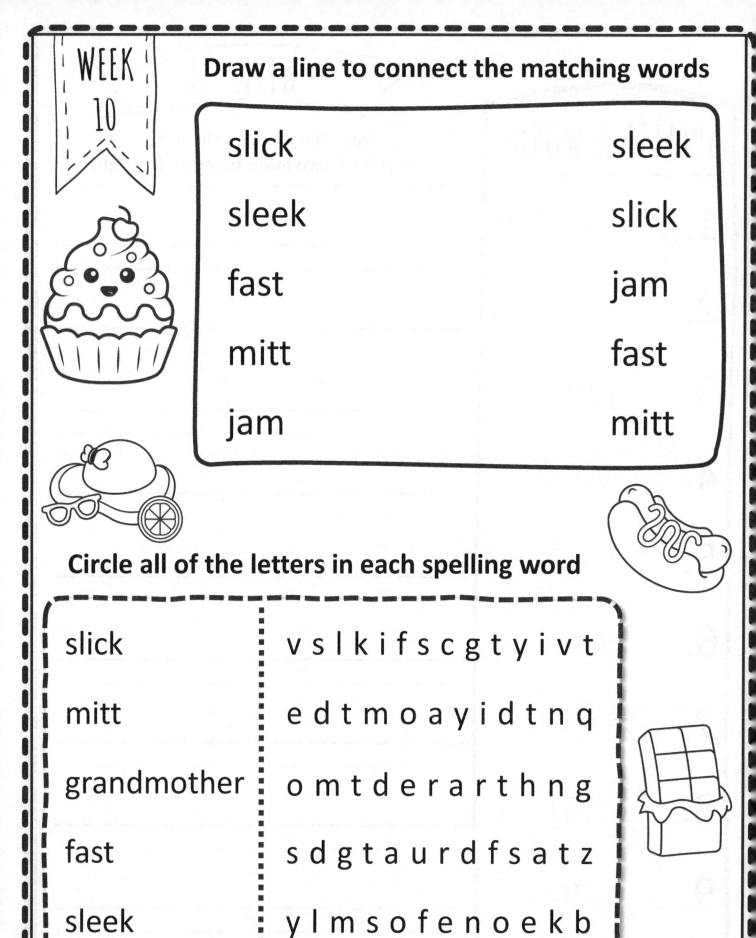

Use different colors to fill in each of the spelling word letters.

slick

sleek

grandmother

fast

right

mitt

jam

pine

chest

went

WEEK 10

FIND EACH SPELLING WORD IN THE WORDSEARCH BELOW

J	M	P	S	F	W	T	E	M	Z	K	H
R	P	I	S	J	T	I	A	R	E	T	D
I	Z	E	L	D	S	T	N	E	K	P	G
G	I	L	I	I	E	Y	L	H	D	W	T
H	L	N	C	S	H	S	F	T	H	T	S
T	A	E	K	O	C	Z	W	O	I	N	A
J	C	O	J	U	Y	P	Z	M	B	K	F
W	J	E	U	T	V	E	K	D	R	K	S
P	E	W	X	X	X	P	I	N	E	K	U
C	J	N	O	K	V	B	I	A	D	J	F
M	G	F	T	A	K	O	I	R	N	A	S
C	V	X	W	T	N	D	F	G	G	M	T

SLICK

RIGHT

PINE

WENT

SLEEK

GRANDMOTHER

CHEST

FAST

MITT

JAM

Write the correct spelling word for each picture

SPELLING WORDS

Trace the word on the left,
then write it two more times on the right.

1. bright

2. sent

3. grow

4. sight

5. clear

6. yard

7. says

8. tray

9. glass

10. minus

Use the clues below to fill out the crossword with spelling words

Across

2. She _____ hello

3. To increase in size

4. Sunglasses help with this

6. They _____ an email

8. To subtract

9. Find grass here

Down

1. Not blurry

2. To be able to see

5. This can shatter

7. Use this to carry things

Put all of the spelling words in alphabetical order

1. _____
2. _____
3. _____
4. _____
5. _____
6. _____
7. _____
8. _____
9. _____
10. _____

Unscramble the words. Write the correct spelling in the box

igths

imnus

ihtrgb

ryda

raty

Use the words below to complete the sentences

minus   bright   clear

_____

I had to _____ my throat.

Twenty _____ twelve is eight.

At night the stars are very _____ .

Start at any letter and move forward or backward around the circle to find one of the spelling words.
Circle the first letter then write the full word below.

g
h   **1**   i
t   s

c
r   **2**   l
a   e

_____

t
b   **3**   h
r   g
    i

l
a   **4**   g
s   s

u
s   **5**   n
m   i

_____   _____   _____

SPELLING WORDS

Trace the word on the left,
then write it two more times on the right.

1. yellow

2. sail

3. straw

4. crook

5. goat

6. twist

7. shore

8. slant

9. clock

10. after

**Use the letters to complete the word.
Some letters can be used more than once.
Make sure to trace the full word.**

g e l o w t i

t s t

s r a

y i w

a t

Draw pictures of your favorite spelling words and then label them

Use the key to find the hidden spelling words

WEEK 12

A	B	C	D	E	F	G	H	I	J	K	L	M
14	10	2	9	18	7	22	8	16	24	13	20	26

N	O	P	Q	R	S	T	U	V	W	X	Y	Z
25	5	3	1	17	12	11	4	19	15	23	6	21

  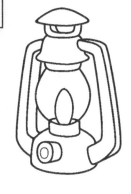

1 6 18 20 20 5 15

2 12 11 17 14 15

3 12 14 16 20

_____

4 2 17 5 5 13

5 22 5 14 11

6 11 15 16 12 11

_____

7 12 8 5 17 18

8 2 20 5 2 13

9 12 20 14 25 11

_____

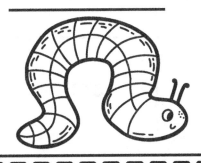

10 14 7 11 18 17

_____

Write the correct spelling for each image

before →

① _____

③ _____

② _____

④ _____

1. Circle the correctly spelled words
2. Rewrite the incorrect words on the lines to the left

① _____

② _____

③ _____

④ _____

clock	crook	slent
twist	yullow	straw
aftre	shure	sail

SPELLING WORDS

Trace the word on the left,
then write it two more times on the right.

1. tooth

2. soon

3. rabbit

4. push

5. stood

6. where

7. stone

8. lock

9. could

10. goes

WEEK 13

Can you help fill each jar with honey?
Write a spelling word on each.

Unscramble the words and write the correct spelling on the line

thoto _____

oosn _____

btriab _____

suph _____

dtoos _____

wrehe _____

ntose _____

codul _____

Draw a line to connect the matching words

where   goes

stone   lock

lock   stone

could   where

goes   could

Circle the correct spelling of each word below

1. tuuth   toothe   tooth   tuoth

2. rabbet   rabbut   rabit   rabbit

3. could   culd   cood   cuuld

4. stuud   stood   stoud   stoud

Use the words below to complete the sentences

lock   stone   rabbit   tooth   could   soon

Did your _____ come out?

This is my pet _____ .

Did you _____ the front door?

This table is made of _____ .

My mom _____ be home _____ .

SPELLING WORDS

Trace the word on the left,
then write it two more times on the right.

1. mother

2. pain

3. speech

4. food

5. spoke

6. toad

7. warm

8. duck

9. mess

10. always

WEEK 14

FIND EACH SPELLING WORD IN THE WORDSEARCH BELOW

L	A	N	G	B	F	Q	C	M	M	K	O
T	X	L	Q	F	B	O	R	D	P	G	F
F	R	H	W	A	V	M	E	S	S	F	N
O	A	H	S	A	S	C	H	I	B	G	N
O	P	V	D	A	Y	A	T	O	Y	T	H
D	F	H	C	U	F	S	O	F	O	K	C
J	N	E	S	Q	C	P	M	A	H	C	E
N	C	Q	J	X	V	K	D	Y	W	A	E
E	B	R	M	T	V	R	S	N	B	W	P
N	E	K	O	P	S	W	A	Q	O	W	S
U	N	A	O	H	H	L	Q	E	C	H	Y
P	A	I	N	W	W	A	R	M	K	J	I

ALWAYS

MESS

DUCK

WARM

TOAD

SPOKE

FOOD

SPEECH

PAIN

MOTHER

Write the correct spelling word for each picture

Start at any letter and move around the circle, forward or backward, to find one of the spelling words.
Circle the first letter then write the full word below

1 h t e o r m

2 a w r m

3 y a s w a l

4 s h p c e e

5 s p e o k

_____   _____

_____   _____   _____

Use the words below to complete the sentences

mess   always   mother   warm   food

Do not make a _____ with your _____.

It is very _____ outside today!

She will _____ love her _____.

Put all of the spelling words in alphabetical order

Unscramble the words. Write the correct spelling in the box

cukd

osekp

ofod

hsepec

npai

1. _____

2. _____

3. _____

4. _____

5. _____

6. _____

7. _____

8. _____

9. _____

10. _____

SPELLING WORDS

Trace the word on the left,
then write it two more times on the right.

1. sand

2. kiss

3. summer

4. speed

5. brother

6. blink

7. downtown

8. grape

9. sheep

10. drive

WEEK 15

Circle all of the letters in each spelling word

sand	n s n k i j a c t u d q
kiss	p d k s o e a v n i m s
brother	k r t d c q o e t h b r
blink	s b g i a i l r n f s k u
downtown	x d z o a y w e d t n s

Put the following words in their correct shape boxes

sand   grape   summer

Circle the spelling words to help the ladybug get ice cream.

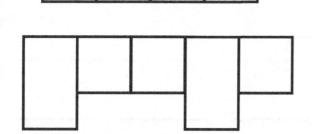

	sand	blink	yes
verb	wow	brother	sheep
wow	pill	news	kiss
swim	screw	speed	hit
read	summer	two	undo
water	downtown	road	trip
jump	grape	drive	

Use the words below to complete the sentences

sand   summer   blink   drive   grape   brother

Their _____ is old enough to _____ .

This medicine is a _____ flavor.

My favorite season of the year is _____ .

If you _____ you might miss it.

At the beach I got _____ between my toes.

Unscramble the words and write the correct spelling on the line

erivd _____   bilkn _____

pseeh _____   hrbeotr _____

rgaep _____   epdes _____

tnwwodno _____   umsemr _____

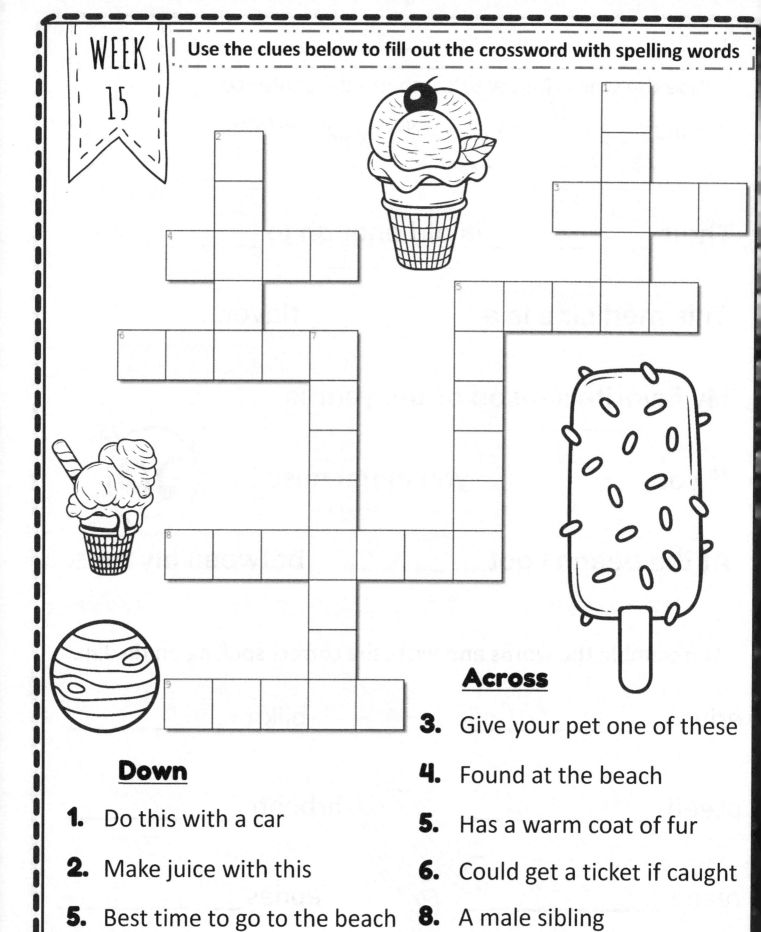

WEEK 15

Use the clues below to fill out the crossword with spelling words

Across

3. Give your pet one of these

4. Found at the beach

5. Has a warm coat of fur

6. Could get a ticket if caught

8. A male sibling

9. Your eyelids do this

Down

1. Do this with a car

2. Make juice with this

5. Best time to go to the beach

7. Center of a city

SPELLING WORDS

Trace the word on the left,
then write it two more times on the right.

1. seal

2. away

3. ago

4. plate

5. would

6. treat

7. angry

8. brand

9. wash

10. heard

Write the correct spelling for each image

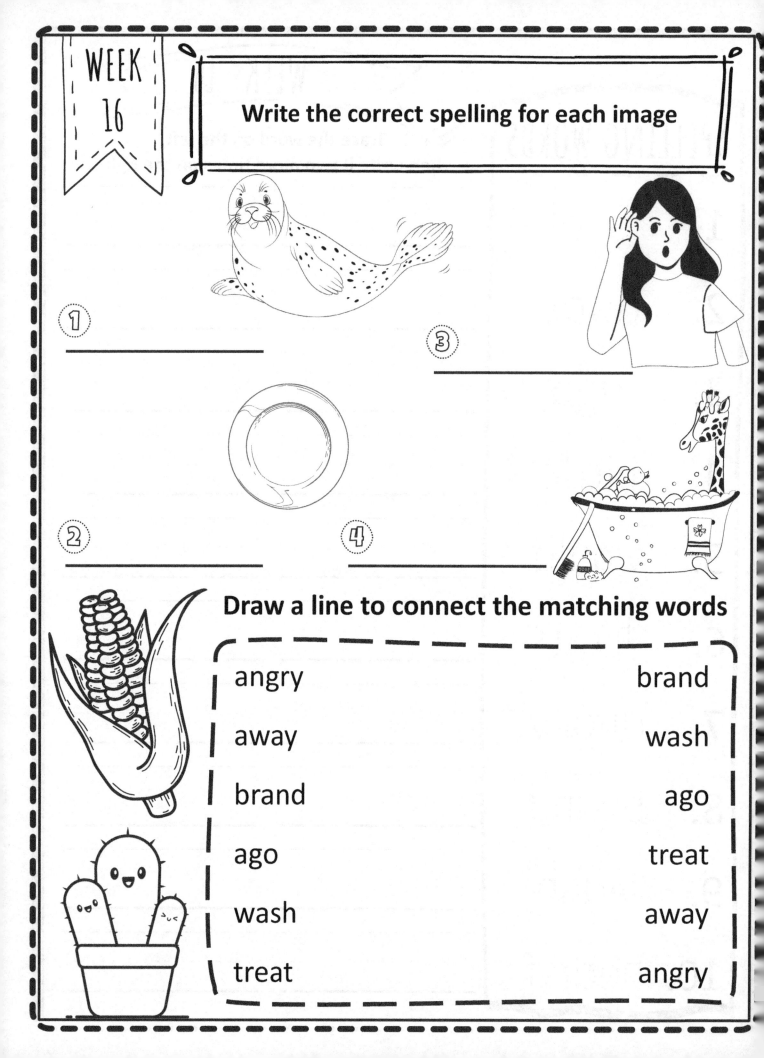

① _____

② _____

③ _____

④ _____

Draw a line to connect the matching words

angry	brand
away	wash
brand	ago
ago	treat
wash	away
treat	angry

Put all of the spelling words in alphabetical order

WEEK 16

1. _____

2. _____

3. _____

4. _____

5. _____

6. _____

7. _____

8. _____

9. _____

10. _____

Unscramble the words. Write the correct spelling in the box

drhea

dbanr

ngrya

lodwu

aywa

Use the letters to complete the word.
Some letters can be used more than once.
Make sure to trace the full word.

h e n a d r s

e _ _ _ _ _ _ _ h _ r

b a d _ _ _ _ _ w _ h

Put the following words in their correct shape boxes

treat   plate   ago   would

SPELLING WORDS

1. animal
2. those
3. click
4. tug
5. blimp
6. mitten
7. made
8. gloss
9. globe
10. camp

Trace the word on the left,
then write it two more times on the right.

WEEK 17

Write a spelling word from this week on any available space on turtle's shell below.

Use the key to find the hidden spelling words

A	B	C	D	E	F	G	H	I	J	K	L	M
14	10	2	9	18	7	22	8	16	24	13	20	26

N	O	P	Q	R	S	T	U	V	W	X	Y	Z
25	5	3	1	17	12	11	4	19	15	23	6	21

1) 2 14 26 3

_____

2) 26 16 11 11 18 25

_____

3) 26 14 9 18

_____

4) 10 20 16 26 3

_____

5) 22 20 5 12 12

_____

6) 22 20 5 10 18

_____

7) 11 4 22

_____

8) 2 20 16 2 13

_____

9) 14 25 16 26 14 20

_____

10) 11 8 5 12 18

_____

WEEK 17

FIND EACH SPELLING WORD IN THE WORDSEARCH BELOW

X	V	U	T	M	Z	S	U	W	Y	X	I
P	H	A	N	I	M	A	L	N	G	G	D
B	R	E	S	P	T	P	K	Z	X	L	W
K	L	N	S	Y	M	F	C	E	N	O	M
C	T	C	O	I	Z	C	D	H	S	B	I
I	X	U	L	I	L	A	E	C	D	E	T
L	V	B	G	T	M	M	D	K	V	M	T
C	C	Z	K	C	Q	P	E	D	I	Q	E
Q	Z	C	X	M	H	P	J	N	S	G	N
T	R	E	S	O	H	T	D	Z	Y	L	O
T	V	A	B	V	Y	J	Y	S	Z	R	U
T	J	E	K	A	E	G	G	C	V	O	V

ANIMAL

THOSE

CLICK

CAMP

BLIMP

MITTEN

MADE

GLOSS

GLOBE

TUG

Write the correct spelling for each picture

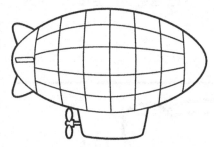

_____ _____

WEEK 18

SPELLING WORDS

Trace the word on the left,
then write it two more times on the right.

1. family
2. stick
3. sea
4. flung
5. zebra
6. smart
7. cannot
8. send
9. while
10. doctor

WEEK 18

Color in the circles you need to spell each word in the box.
Unscramble the leftover circles to spell a word from this week.

T

doctor   while   cannot   zebra   family   flung

F I O C W O R T D
M N Y N R S I
C E T B L G Z F
A M H O A U N A E
R L

Write the hidden word here:

_____

Use the words below to complete the sentences

send   sea   stick   family

_____

I will _____ a letter in the mail.

_____

Many fish live in the _____ .

_____ should always _____ together.

Look at the letters in the shapes and then answer the questions below.

r
o
c
t
o
i
e
w
d
s
n
e
h
l

1. What spelling word can you make from the letters in the square? _____

2. What spelling word can you make from the letters in the circle? _____

3. What spelling word can you make from the letters outside of both shapes? _____

Circle this week's correct spelling word in each row

1.	fluung	fllung	flung	flunge
2.	zebra	zebraa	zebrah	zebruh
3.	smarte	smart	smert	smartt
4.	stieck	stiick	stikc	stick

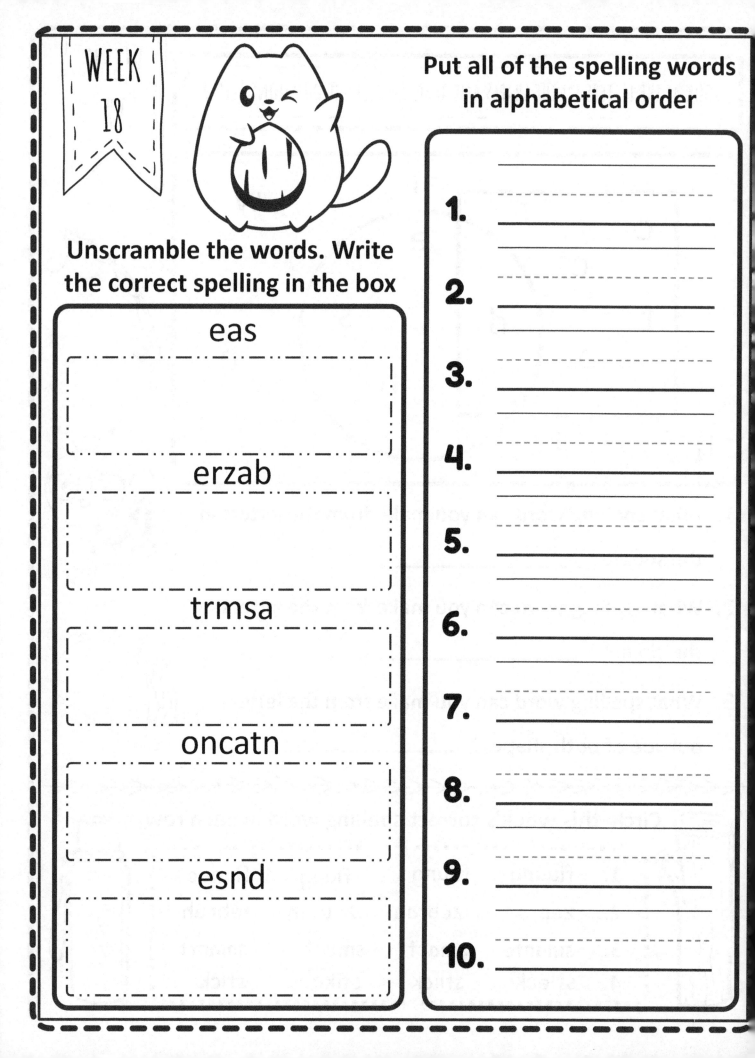

Put all of the spelling words in alphabetical order

Unscramble the words. Write the correct spelling in the box

eas

erzab

trmsa

oncatn

esnd

1.

2.

3.

4.

5.

6.

7.

8.

9.

10.

SPELLING WORDS

Trace the word on the left,
then write it two more times on the right.

1. clapped

2. flash

3. toast

4. drum

5. bean

6. under

7. swine

8. path

9. sleet

10. feed

FIND EACH SPELLING WORD IN THE WORDSEARCH BELOW

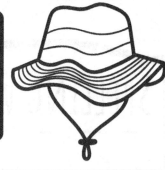

V	K	M	T	O	T	N	L	O	S	G	T
F	X	M	R	E	L	F	G	L	O	V	O
U	L	H	S	B	D	D	E	X	I	H	D
B	E	A	N	F	R	E	D	N	U	A	Y
A	U	S	S	F	T	P	Z	C	W	L	T
M	N	F	Y	H	X	P	G	H	R	N	H
U	K	E	T	C	O	A	V	L	X	N	W
R	I	E	O	A	C	L	S	W	I	N	E
D	F	D	A	G	J	C	R	W	V	C	H
P	E	J	S	Z	N	J	H	F	R	W	T
D	N	D	T	W	W	S	M	B	G	T	A
P	P	O	D	Q	V	O	O	Y	L	N	P

FLASH

TOAST

CLAPPED

DRUM

BEAN

UNDER

SWINE

PATH

SLEET

FEED

As you find each spelling word write it below

_____   _____   _____

_____   _____   _____

Use the words below to complete the sentences

feed   clapped   under   toast   path

_____   _____

The _____ went _____ the bridge.

_____

Peanut butter on _____ is delicious.

_____

The crowd _____ after the show.

_____

Please do not forget to _____ your dog.

Draw a picture of four different spelling words
from this week then label them

UNSCRAMBLE THE WORDS AND WRITE THE CORRECT SPELLING ON THE LINE

eltse _____

adpepcl _____

enisw _____

totsa _____

redun _____

asfhl _____

Start at any letter and move around the circle, forward or backward, to find one of the spelling words. Circle the first letter then write the full word below

a
p   l
1
p   c
e   d

a
n   **2**   e
b

_____

_____

t
t
3   s
o
a

f
h   **4**   l
s   a

s
w   **5**   e
i   n

_____

SPELLING WORDS

Trace the word on the left,
then write it two more times on the right.

1. choke
2. raise
3. grade
4. stain
5. trim
6. every
7. caught
8. lump
9. yet
10. pool

Color in the circles you need to spell each word in the box.
Unscramble the leftover circles to spell a word from this week

| choke | raise | pool | lump | every | trim |

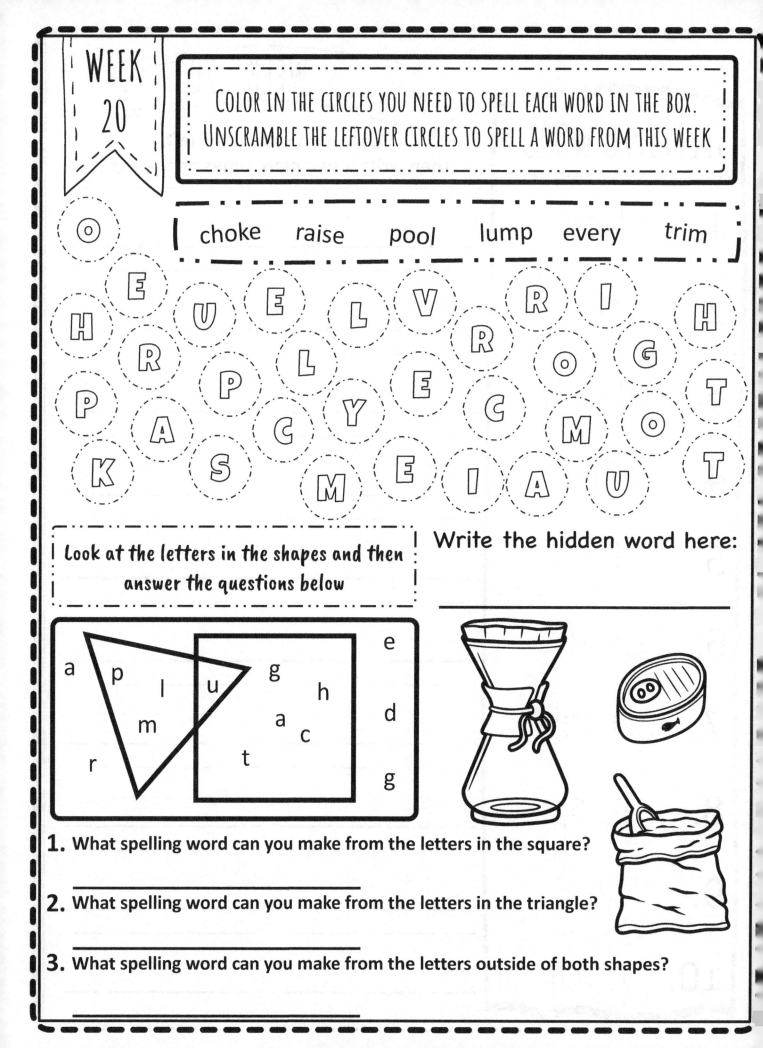

Look at the letters in the shapes and then answer the questions below

Write the hidden word here:

_____

1. What spelling word can you make from the letters in the square?

_____

2. What spelling word can you make from the letters in the triangle?

_____

3. What spelling word can you make from the letters outside of both shapes?

_____

Use the words below to complete the sentences

grade   every   choke   yet   pool

_____ summer I swim in a _____ .

I am not in high school, _____ !

I got the highest _____ in my class!

Please eat slower so you do not _____ .

1. Circle the correctly spelled words
2. Rewrite the incorrect words on the lines to the left

① _____

② _____

③ _____

④ _____

evury	lump	trim
cuaght	grayde	raize
pool	stain	choke

SPELLING WORDS

Trace the word on the left,
then write it two more times on the right.

1. their

2. boot

3. across

4. between

5. slid

6. bath

7. bead

8. fight

9. thrift

10. flesh

FIND EACH SPELLING WORD IN THE WORDSEARCH BELOW

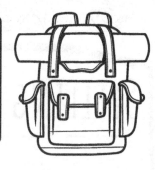

S	R	F	B	O	O	T	F	W	W	H	E
N	U	T	I	B	N	A	R	N	H	F	U
Z	J	H	Y	G	Q	M	J	E	L	E	M
T	R	E	A	A	H	S	V	E	J	N	I
B	X	I	P	M	G	T	S	W	J	L	T
T	H	R	I	F	T	H	Z	T	Z	L	D
S	S	O	R	C	A	U	X	E	I	I	P
A	S	F	D	W	C	N	C	B	L	X	T
G	Z	M	W	A	L	N	U	S	H	V	C
H	T	A	B	O	E	E	C	M	M	S	S
X	U	J	V	P	Y	B	U	B	J	U	A
C	G	W	B	H	Q	Y	S	Z	Q	D	G

THEIR

BOOT

ACROSS

BETWEEN

SLID

BATH

BEAD

FIGHT

THRIFT

FLESH

 As you find each spelling word write it below

_____   _____   _____

_____   _____   _____

Put all of the spelling words in alphabetical order

1. _____

2. _____

3. _____

4. _____

5. _____

6. _____

7. _____

8. _____

9. _____

10. _____

Unscramble the words. Write the correct spelling in the box

adbe

hbta

dils

ewetebn

coarss

Use the letters to complete the word.
Some letters can be used more than once.
Make sure to trace the full word.

e i l t b f h s

t___r   f___h

h r___t   ___oo

Put the following words in their correct shape boxes

between   slid   fight   bead

SPELLING WORDS

Trace the word on the left,
then write it two more times on the right.

1. blast

2. seen

3. bring

4. owl

5. chore

6. dust

7. clean

8. father

9. maybe

10. goose

Draw a line to connect the matching words

goose	dust
bring	maybe
chore	chore
maybe	father
dust	goose
father	bring

Circle all of the letters in each spelling word

blast	s l b i f s a d t y f w t
clean	e c t m l a y i e t n a
owl	o m t w e r l r t w n l
seen	s d g t e u r d e s a n z
chore	y r m s r f e h o e k c

Use the key to find the hidden spelling words

A	B	C	D	E	F	G	H	I	J	K	L	M
14	10	2	9	18	7	22	8	16	24	13	20	26

N	O	P	Q	R	S	T	U	V	W	X	Y	Z
25	5	3	1	17	12	11	4	19	15	23	6	21

1. 10 20 14 12 11

2. 22 5 5 12 18

3. 12 18 18 25

_____

_____

_____

4. 26 14 6 10 18

5. 10 17 16 25 22

6. 2 8 5 17 18

_____

_____

_____

7. 5 15 20

8. 9 4 12 11

9. 7 14 11 8 18 17

_____

_____

_____

10. 2 20 18 14 25

_____

SPELLING WORDS

Trace the word on the left,
then write it two more times on the right.

1. tiger

2. shock

3. why

4. soap

5. been

6. dash

7. dock

8. boat

9. spy

10. park

WEEK 23

FIND EACH SPELLING WORD IN THE WORDSEARCH BELOW

G	T	K	C	O	H	S	S	N	R	Z	O
N	G	C	D	L	V	G	P	T	E	P	L
E	K	A	Q	H	E	A	O	T	F	M	T
E	C	K	S	T	U	A	P	A	R	K	C
B	O	A	J	I	B	F	B	R	W	F	L
X	D	E	T	J	E	T	I	G	E	R	U
H	O	L	F	Q	R	P	A	O	S	L	U
X	O	B	J	B	L	H	C	F	O	Y	H
E	C	C	U	Y	O	W	W	Y	Y	O	I
M	C	H	Y	Q	P	A	X	Y	C	H	K
L	A	T	L	M	U	S	T	Q	G	B	W
G	W	O	X	U	Q	I	B	W	P	O	G

TIGER

SHOCK

WHY

SOAP

BEEN

DASH

DOCK

BOAT

SPY

PARK

 **As you find each spelling word write it below**

_____ _____ _____

_____ _____ _____

Look at the letters in the shapes and then answer the questions below

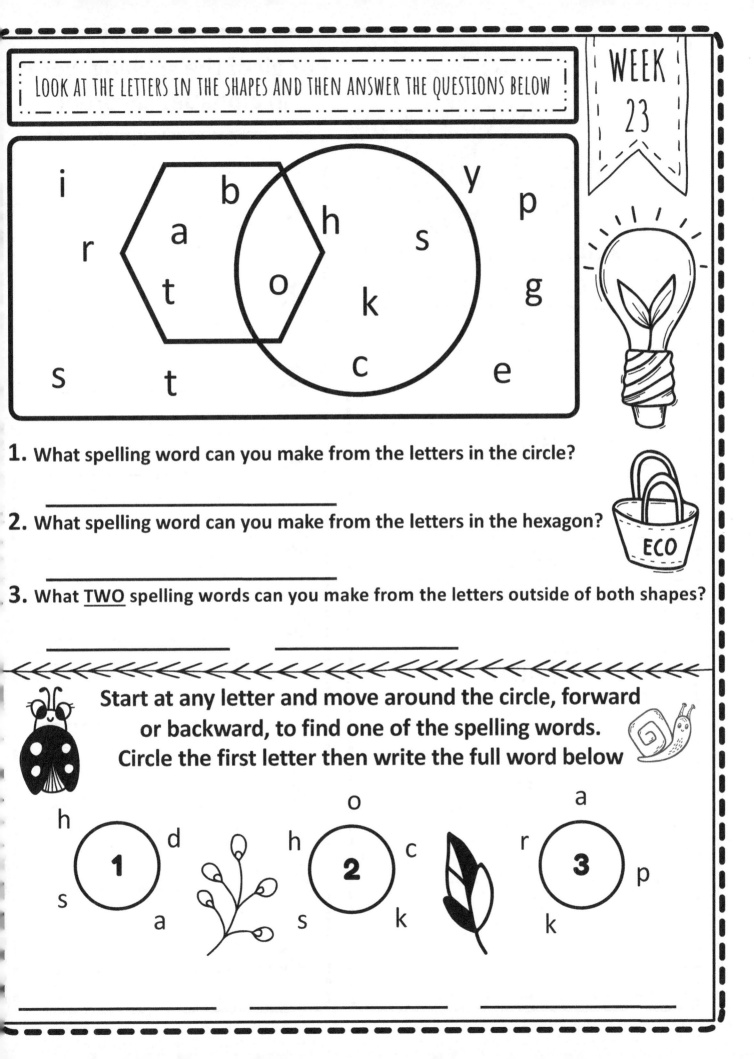

i r s

b a t t

h o k c

y p s g e

1. What spelling word can you make from the letters in the circle?

_____

2. What spelling word can you make from the letters in the hexagon?

_____

3. What __TWO__ spelling words can you make from the letters outside of both shapes?

_____   _____

Start at any letter and move around the circle, forward or backward, to find one of the spelling words. Circle the first letter then write the full word below

h d **1** s a

o h **2** c s k

a r **3** p k

_____   _____

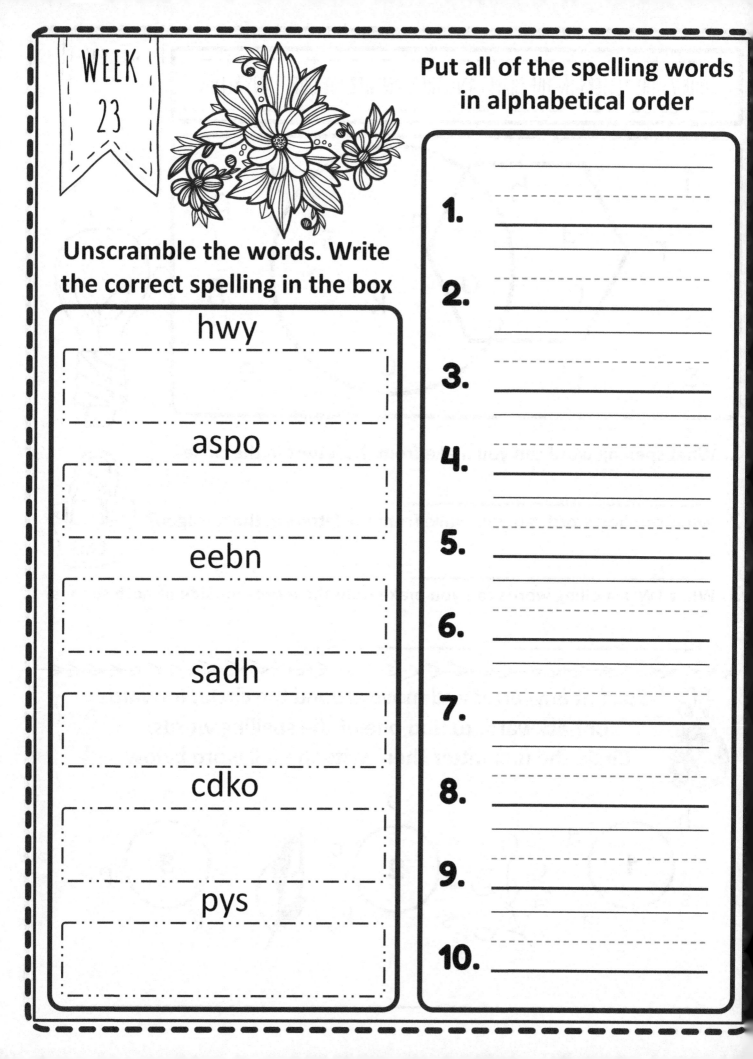

WEEK 23

Unscramble the words. Write the correct spelling in the box

hwy

aspo

eebn

sadh

cdko

pys

Put all of the spelling words in alphabetical order

1. _____

2. _____

3. _____

4. _____

5. _____

6. _____

7. _____

8. _____

9. _____

10. _____

SPELLING WORDS

Trace the word on the left,
then write it two more times on the right.

1. cash

2. flight

3. vase

4. blow

5. better

6. outside

7. loud

8. these

9. cookie

10. snack

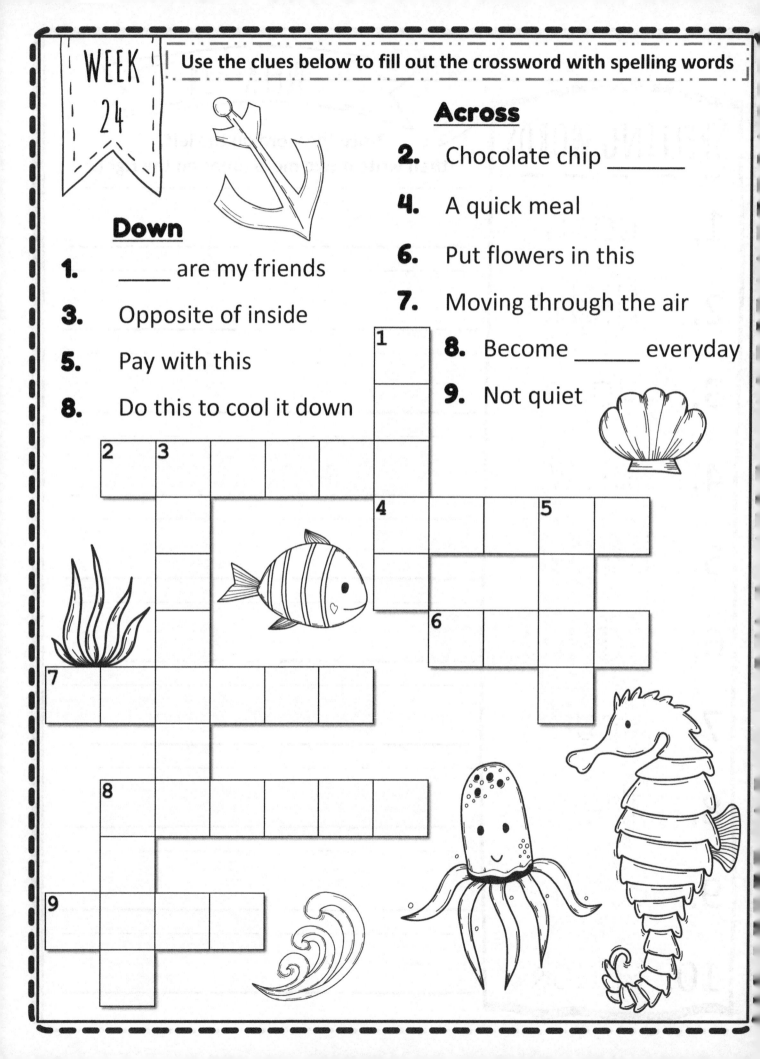

WEEK 24

Use the clues below to fill out the crossword with spelling words

Across

2. Chocolate chip _____

4. A quick meal

6. Put flowers in this

7. Moving through the air

8. Become _____ everyday

9. Not quiet

Down

1. _____ are my friends

3. Opposite of inside

5. Pay with this

8. Do this to cool it down

Use the words below to complete the sentences

outside   better   loud   cookie   vase   cash

Music at a rock concert is very _____ .

The corner store only accepts _____ .

This _____ just came out of the oven.

I am feeling _____ , can I play _____ ?

Put all of the flowers in the blue _____ .

Unscramble the words and write the correct spelling on the line

estdoiu _____   hasc _____

etesh _____   gltifh _____

okecio _____   svae _____

scnka _____   ttrebe _____

Color in the circles you need to spell each word in the box.
Unscramble the leftover circles to spell a word from this week.

flight   blow   better   outside   these   snack

L   E

F   E   T   O   S   I   I   W   I   H

O   U   L   T   K   D   S   R   B

A   E   C   E   C   N   E   B   E

G   K   T   O   H   T   S   O   T

Write the hidden word here:

_____

Circle this week's correct spelling word in each row

1.	loude	louud	loud	loudd
2.	flyt	flyht	flyte	flight
3.	theese	these	thees	theze
4.	better	bettr	bettur	beetur
5.	snakee	snaak	snakc	snack

SPELLING WORDS

Trace the word on the left,
then write it two more times on the right.

1. bread

2. hook

3. stamp

4. flaw

5. live

6. wheel

7. bang

8. steep

9. before

10. fish

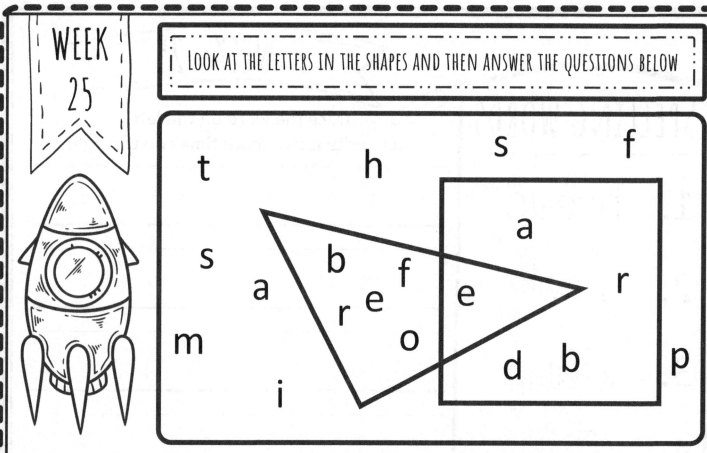

1. What spelling word can you make from the letters in the triangle?

_____

2. What spelling word can you make from the letters in the square?

_____

3. What **TWO** spelling words can you make from the letters outside of both shapes?

_____   _____

Start at any letter and move around the circle, forward
or backward, to find one of the spelling words.
Circle the first letter then write the full word below

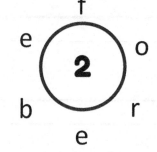

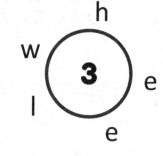

_____   _____   _____

Find each spelling word in the wordsearch below

D	B	B	D	W	K	U	D	Q	N	P	S
W	M	V	R	K	Q	K	Q	B	U	F	H
J	F	D	L	E	P	I	Y	Z	X	E	Q
K	H	C	I	W	A	M	R	F	I	R	Y
F	W	E	V	H	K	D	A	M	I	S	J
I	A	D	E	E	K	E	P	T	Q	S	O
N	L	J	V	E	O	P	U	E	S	O	H
H	F	U	G	L	E	E	C	J	E	G	S
O	P	Z	C	Y	C	O	E	U	P	T	B
O	Q	N	V	M	E	I	U	M	N	S	S
K	U	X	B	E	F	O	R	E	C	E	R
X	G	T	P	L	L	B	Z	B	A	N	G

BREAD

HOOK

STAMP

FLAW

LIVE

WHEEL

BANG

STEEP

BEFORE

FISH

As you find each spelling word write it below

--- --- ---

--- --- ---

--- --- ---

WEEK 25

This panda needs help writing a spelling word from this week on each balloon. Can you help?

MORE WRITING PRACTICE!

Trace the word on the left, then write it at least three more times on the right.

BONUS

1. summer

2. downtown

3. brother

4. bright

5. twelve

6. yesterday

7. found

8. upon

9. yellow

10. rabbit

Answer Key

We 🤍 trees, which is why we've made the answer key digital.

Visit the below link to easily download it:

https://bit.ly/3JepPaH

Bonus

Leave this book a review and
we may send you something special.

Made in the USA
Monee, IL
21 November 2023

46998581R00059